RUBANK
Treasures

for TROMBONE (BARITONE B.C.)

PLAYBACK+
Speed • Pitch • Balance • Loop

CONTENTS

To access recordings and PDF piano accompaniments, go to:
www.halleonard.com/mylibrary

Enter Code
3517-5875-6057-4361

ISBN 978-1-4803-5255-1

RUBANK®

HAL•LEONARD®
7777 W. BLUEMOUND RD. P.O. BOX 13819 MILWAUKEE, WI 53213

Visit Hal Leonard Online at
www.halleonard.com

American Patrol

1st Trombone/Baritone B.C. (Solo)

F.W. Meacham
Arranged by Herman A. Hummel

00121448

American Patrol

2nd Trombone/Baritone B.C. (Duet)

F.W. Meacham
Arranged by Herman A. Hummel

00121448

Andante and Allegro

Trombone/Baritone B.C.

Robert Clérisse
Edited by H. Voxman

Ave Maria
(Ellens Gesang III, D. 839)

Trombone/Baritone B.C.

Franz Schubert
Arranged by Clair W. Johnson

Air Gai

Trombone/Baritone B.C.

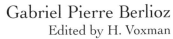

Gabriel Pierre Berlioz
Edited by H. Voxman

00121448

Piano

rall.

Prayer
from *Cavalleria Rusticana*

Trombone/Baritone B.C.

Pietro Mascagni
Arranged by Clair W. Johnson

00121448

Toreador's Song
from *Carmen*

Trombone/Baritone B.C.

Georges Bizet
Arranged by G.E. Holmes

Air and Variations on a Civil War Song
("Tramp, Tramp, Tramp")

Trombone/Baritone B.C.

George F. Root
Arranged by E. DeLamater

00121448

Jabberwocky

Trombone/Baritone B.C.

Harold L. Walters

00121448

13

00121448

Prélude et Divertissement

Trombone/Baritone B.C.

Robert Clérisse
Edited by H. Voxman

00121448

Aria and Allegro

Trombone/Baritone B.C.

Franz Joseph Haydn
Transcribed by H. Voxman

Largo assai e con espressione
[Slow four]

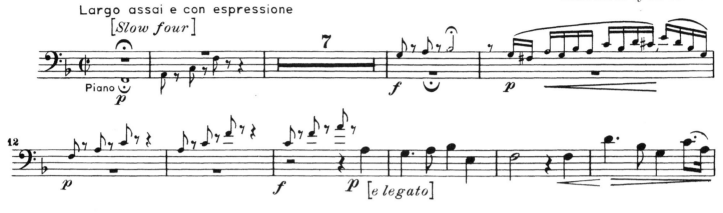

Allegro

00121448

Orientale

Trombone/Baritone B.C.

J.Ed. Barat
Edited by H. Voxman

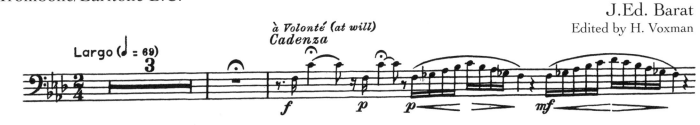

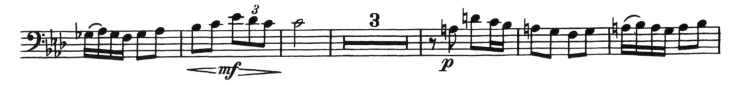

* Designates a recording "click"
(accomp. recording only)

00121448

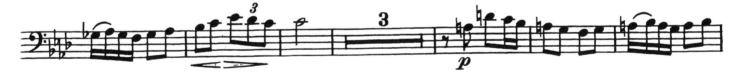

Concerto in F Minor

Trombone/Baritone B.C.

Émile Lauga
EDITED BY H. Voxman

00121448

21

00121448

Lyric Interlude

Trombone/Baritone B.C.

Clair W. Johnson

† Each * designates an eighth-note "click"
(accomp. recording only)

Summer Serenade

Trombone/Baritone B.C.

Clarence E. Hurrell

00121448